PRESENT COMPANY

ALSO BY W.S. MERWIN

W.S. MERWIN

Present Company

COPPER CANYON PRESS

Printed in the United States of America

Cover art: Adam Fuss, from the series *In Between*, 1994. Cibachrome photogram. Copyright by Adam Fuss. Courtesy Cheim & Read, New York City.

Present Company is set in Scala, a font designed by Martin Majoor. Book design and composition by Valerie Brewster, Scribe Typography. Printed on archival-quality paper at McNaughton & Gunn, Inc.

Copper Canyon Press is in residence at Fort Worden State Park in Port Townsend, Washington, under the auspices of Centrum Foundation. Centrum is a gathering place for artists and creative thinkers from around the world, students of all ages and backgrounds, and audiences seeking extraordinary cultural enrichment.

LIBRARY OF CONGRESS CATALOGING-IN-PUBLICATION DATA

Merwin, W.S. (William Stanley), 1927–
Present company / W.S. Merwin.
    p. cm.
ISBN 1-55659-227-2 (alk. paper)
    I. Title.
PS3563.E75P74 2005
811'.54—DC22   2005008867

9 8 7 6 5 4 3 2

FIRST PRINTING

COPPER CANYON PRESS
Post Office Box 271
Port Townsend, Washington 98368

www.coppercanyonpress.org

To
Matt and Karen
and to
John and Aleksandra
beloved present company

ACKNOWLEDGMENTS

Grateful acknowledgment is made to the editors of the following publications, in which a number of these poems first appeared:

The American Poetry Review: "To This May," "To a Reflection," "To the Face in the Mirror," "To the Tongue," "To a Friend Travelling," "To _____," "To Duty," "To My Mother," "To the Middle," "To Purity," "To Salt," "To the Gods," "To Finding Again," "To Days of Winter," "To the Morning (2)," "To the Story," and "To the Parting Year."

The Atlantic Monthly: "To Age," "To My Teeth," "To Smoke," and "To a Tortoiseshell Lyre."

Conjunctions, Howard Norman guest editor: "To the Shadow."

The Nation: "To the Margin," "To Being Late," and "To the Unfinished."

The New York Review of Books: "To the Knife," "To the Present Visitors," "To My Father's Houses," "To Monday," and "To the Happy Few."

The New Yorker: "To the Soul," "To Waiting," "To Impatience," "To the Sorrow String," "To the Words," "To the Grass of Autumn," "To Ashes," "To Zbigniew Herbert's Bicycle," "To Forgetting," "To Myself," and "To the Book."

The Paris Review: "To History" and "To the Unlikely Event."

Poetry: "To Lingering Regrets," "To the Consolations of Philosophy," "To Absence," "To a Few Cherries," "To the Mistakes," "To Luck," "To the Blank Spaces," "To the Light of September," and "To the Fire."

The Yale Review: "To Lili's Walk" and "To My Grandfathers."

Contents

PRESENT COMPANY

To This May

They know so much more now about
the heart we are told but the world
still seems to come one at a time
one day one year one season and here
it is spring once more with its birds
nesting in the holes in the walls
its morning finding the first time
its light pretending not to move
always beginning as it goes

To the Soul

Is anyone there
if so
are you real
either way are you
one or several
if the latter
are you all at once
or do you
take turns not answering

is your answer
the question itself
surviving the asking
without end
whose question is it
how does it begin
where does it come from
how did it ever
find out about you
over the sound
of itself
with nothing but its own
ignorance to go by

To a Reflection

You are what we believe
even if we know better
seeing is believing
though you write backwards
your left our right
so that we never can read you
if there is any message
directed toward us from

the other side which we
cannot touch cannot reach
and can see only from here
where there is something you seem
to be showing us over
and over again without
a sound as though you were
the light itself returning

apparently to the same place

To the Face in the Mirror

Because you keep turning toward me
what I suppose must be
my own features only
backward it seems to me
that you are able to see
me only by
looking back from somewhere
that is a picture of here
at this moment but
reversed and already
not anywhere

so how far
away are you
after all who seem to be
so near and eternally
out of reach
you with the white hair
now who still surprise me
day after day
staring back at me
out of nowhere
past present or future
you with no weight or name
no will of your own
and the sight of me
shining in your eye

how do you
know it is me

To Waiting

You spend so much of your time
expecting to become
someone else
always someone
who will be different
someone to whom a moment
whatever moment it may be
at last has come
and who has been
met and transformed
into no longer being you
and so has forgotten you

meanwhile in your life
you hardly notice
the world around you
lights changing
sirens dying along the buildings
your eyes intent
on a sight you do not see yet
not yet there
as long as you
are only yourself

with whom as you
recall you were
never happy
to be left alone for long

To Impatience

Don't wish your life away
my mother said and I saw
past her words that same day
suddenly not there
nor the days after
even the ones I remember

and though hands held back the hounds
on the way to the hunt
now the fleet deer are gone
that bounded before them
all too soon overtaken
as she knew they would be

and well as she warned me
always calling me home
to the moment around me
that was taking its good time
and willingly though I
heeded her words to me
once again waking me
to the breath that was there

you too kept whispering
up close to my ear
the secrets of hunger
for some prize not yet there
sight of face touch of skin
light in another valley
labor triumphant or
last word of a story
without which you insisted

the world would not be complete
soon soon you repeated
it cannot be too soon

yet you know it can
and you know it would be
the end of you too only
if ever it arrives
you find something else missing
and I know I must thank you
for your faithful discontent
and what it has led me to
yes yes you have guided me
but what is hard now to see
is the mortal hurry

To Age

It is time to tell you
what you may have guessed
along the way without
letting it deter you
do you remember how
once you liked to kneel looking
out of the back window
while your father was driving
and the thread then of pleasure
as you watched the world appear
on both sides and from under
you coming together
into place out of nowhere
growing steadily longer
and you would hum to it
not from contentment but
to keep time with no time
floating out along it
seeing the world grow
smaller as it went from you
farther becoming longer
and longer but still there
well it was not like that
but once it was out of sight
it was not anywhere
with the dreams of that night
whether remembered or not
and wherever it was
arriving from on its way
through you must have been growing
shorter even as you

watched it appear and go
you still cannot say how
but you cannot even tell
whether the subway coming
in time out of the tunnel
is emerging from
the past or the future

To Lingering Regrets

Without wanting to
I have come slowly
to admit that I know
who you are one by one
O lovely and mournful
with downcast eyes
appearing to me as
you are turning away
to stand silent and late
in a remembered light
touched with amber
as the sun is going
from a day that it brought
you come to me again
and again to wait
as beautiful as ever
at the edge of the light
you have not changed at all
as far as I can tell
and you learn nothing from me
who do not talk with you
but see you waiting there
without once moving toward you
O forever hopeful
and forever young
you are the foolish virgins
with no oil for your lamps
and no one else to lead you
where you want to go

To My Teeth

So the companions
of Ulysses those that were
still with him after
the nights in the horse the sea-lanes
the other islands the friends
lost one by one in pain
and the coming home one
bare day to a later
age that was their own
but with their scars now upon them
and now darkened and worn and some
broken beyond recognition
and still missing the ones
taken away from beside them
who had grown up with them
and served long without question
wanting nothing else

sat around in the old places
across from the hollows
reminding themselves
that they were the lucky ones
together where they belonged

but would he stay there

To the Ancient Order of Legs

Barefoot all the way
from the embryo
and the drifting sands
where the prints washed away
untold lives ago
you were born to be
one of a number
upholding a larger
company on one
side or the other
always in the infantry
and singular though
at first you were many
balancing alternately
unable to see
where you were going
climbing along yourself
by the numbers in
a pace of your own
and stepping into
new talents positions
memberships bringing
the count down to
eight and four and two
coming in turn to be
less dispensable
half solitary painful
surviving ancestor
heir to the distances
sustain the limbs of friends
you that have borne the world

this far in us all walk on
light on your feet as
the days walk through the days

To My Legs

Tonight I look at you
as of course I never could
and think of the old horses
the little I was told about them

out of gratitude
comes a recognition
of being too late
standing on the empty
platform in the wrong
clothes or none at all
whatever may have been said
before during or afterward

all at once the old horses
were nowhere to be seen
after they had brought us
so far without a word
and I know what happens
to them however
I may pretend not to
a last step into the air
and out of gratitude comes
a picture of nothing

the speechless
obedient journeys
the running in battles
as the fields fall silent
the full veins of youth
gone without a sound

To the Tongue

Whatever we say
we know there is another
language under this one

a word of it is always
there on the tip of you
unsayable and early
O you for whom
all the languages have been named
who have none of your own

naked sleeper in the cave
where you were born
dreamer without words
who first tasted
a verb of the world
you who speak as though
you could see

you have not forgotten
the serpent your ancestor
its fluttering inarticulate flame
of expectation
on the way to you

To the Gift of Sight

What has happened to my eyes
I ask the distances
these days when the light is here
disclosing the late pages
the first leaves of spring
the gray river again
holding the still sky
that shines through it
down in the valley

it is not long ago
that I believed what I saw
without a shadow of doubt
clear contours letters
sharp figures standing for
themselves in my eyes

yet I could see then
how the time kept hiding
moments behind themselves
one after the other
a day at a time
behind the present
and the years were seen only through
each other with their outlines
melting into each other
until they were no longer
immediate or distinct

now those seasons and meanings
inside each other
as one cast a floating

penumbra around themselves
they wear a veil in the light
that makes me prize the glimpse
of them I have
the naked skin of the world
whatever of it can be seen

it uncurls in the cold light
and faces surface
and folded wings
in the water of morning

To the Corner of the Eye

Even now if I
were to call you
you would not come one step closer

though I might
call you my own

attentive companion
never far and never
domesticated
glimpse of the wilderness
in every light
on all sides
nameless familiar

in you a moment
appears before I
can recognize it
yet when I turn to face you
you have stepped aside
leaving me only
the look of things
I once thought I knew

while you are no farther
than you ever were

beginning where I am
with your unseen land
stretching away beyond you
to no horizon

To the Shadow

Only as long as there is light
as long as there is something
a cloud or mountain or wing
or body reflecting the light
you are there on
the other side
twin shape formed of
nothing but absence
made of what you are not
and we recognize you
when we wave
a part of the darkness
waves at the same moment
not answering though
nor mocking us
no
no you are not the self we know
from night to night

To Another William

After most of nine hundred years your words
born of a language that has not been spoken
through more lifetimes than I can imagine
cling to my breath even with its accent
of knowing nothing in a time and place
where anyone who heard you pronounce them
yourself now would not understand what they
were saying all this time as the year turned
new again as the white flower opened
in the cold night as the hands remembered
what they wanted once more as the days grew
few as the one song rose out of nothing

To History

You with a muse of your own
in the old gallery
that profile of grave beauty
still countenance of no
discernible age eyes somewhere

else alighting
afterwards through someone
of whom now we know
nothing but the words from later
indicating a presence
to be wooed bowed to attended
never ignored
                    but she makes

no promises arbiter
of what the speechless
living moment would be
remembered by

she knows you

and knows you are never
the way it was
                    aspect
all in the telling
you were not there at the time
but only in phrases
following each
other looking back

while she says nothing but waits

To the Unlikely Event

You have been evoked so often
like some relative in office
whom we have heard of by name
all these years but have never met

you inhabit a kind of fame
a void without time or senses
beyond anything said of you
so that doubtless you do not hear
the recurring inadequate
references to you which rise
from another age rehearsing
wrong images or none at all

and whenever you may arrive
at last for a visit you come
in pure innocence and too late
to be recognized once you are
here sudden drop in the dials
in the light or the affections
windfall or surprise legacy

but once you come you do not go

how can we ever address you
in your unlikelihood boundless
indifference abroad in your
uncharted self to which only
random syllables find the way
and to what words can we entrust
our groundless hope saying *there there*
to them *how unlikely you sound*

already as though this might be
the mission you were conceived for
it could be what you always meant

and the hope itself when we turn
at the last minute to put it
into words what is there to say
that seems even possible
                                        may
it go on just as it is may
that day never come may it be

spring in the morning together
and without end
                        how unlikely
it sounds when we come to say it

it does not help much to recall
how unlikely it is that we
turned up here with the beginning
strewn around us of which we know
nothing hear nothing remember
only the moment before us
which we believe as it happens
when it appears to be likely

oh be unlikely forever

To a Departing Companion

Only now
I see that you
are the end of spring
cloud passing
across the hollow
of the empty bowl
not making a sound
and the dew is still here

To Lili's Walk

Strange that now there should be no sign of you
visible on the dusty way between
the shadows where the morning light comes through
to lie across those places we have been
time and again though at the other end
of the day when the sun was nearly gone
and from the other side the beams lengthened
under the trees where you kept setting one
foot down carefully before the other
weaving upstream along with me to where
we would go no farther then together
and I said you know the way back from there
I will wait and you can follow alone
and between us the night has come and gone

To a Friend Travelling

The harsh cry of a partridge
echoes along the valley
through the misty rain
two months after you left
you would recognize it
though you no longer noticed the sound
except in your dreams

once again I do not know
where you may be
where to think of you
how to send you anything
whether you need it or not

you may be far away by now
yet I keep hearing your footsteps
all day in the house
in another room
this is like one of those letters
written on a mountain
in China more than
a thousand years ago

by someone staring
at the miles of white clouds
after a friend's departure
there were so many of those
unsigned and never sent
as far as we know

To the Sorrow String

You invisible one
resounding on your own
whatever the others
happen to be playing
source of a note
not there in the score
under whatever key
unphrased continuo
gut stretched between
the beginning and the end
what would the music
be without you
since even through
the chorus of pure joy
the tears hear you
and nothing can restrain them

To _____

There is no reason
for me to keep counting
how long it has been
since you were here
alive one morning

as though I were
letting out the string
of a kite one day at a time
over my finger
when there is no string

To the Consolations of Philosophy

Thank you but
not just at the moment

I know you will say
I have said that before
I know you have been
there all along somewhere
in another time zone

I studied once
those beautiful instructions
when I was young and
far from here
they seemed distant then
they seem distant now
from everything I remember

I hope they stayed with you
when the noose started to tighten
and you could say no more
and after wisdom
and the days in iron
the eyes started from your head

I know the words
must have been set down
partly for yourself
unjustly condemned after
a good life

I know the design
of the world is beyond
our comprehension

thank you
but grief is selfish and in
the present when
the stars do not seem to move
I was not listening

I know it is not
sensible to expect
fortune to grant her
gifts forever
I know

To Grief

O other country
which we never left
rich in anniversaries
each in turn wearing your crown
how many of them are there
like stars returning every one alone
from where they have been all the time
each one the only one
and to whom do you belong
incomparable one

recurring never to be touched again
whether by hand or understanding
familiar presence suddenly approaching
already turned away
reminder hidden
in the names

back of the same sky
that lights the days as we watch them
what do you want it for
this endless longing that is only ours
orbiting even in our syllables
why do you keep calling us as you do
from the beginning without a sound
like a shadow

To Absence

Raw shore of paradise
which the long waves reach
just as they fail
one after the other
bare strand beyond which
at times I believe I see
as in a glass darkly
what I know here
and now cannot be
a face I can never touch
a gaze that cannot stay
which I catch sight of
still turned upon me
following me
from under the sky
of your groundless country
that has no syllable of its own
what good to you
are the treasures beyond
words or number
that you seize forever
unmapped imperium
when only here
in the present
which has lost them
only now
in the moment you
have not yet taken
does anyone know them
or how rare they are

To the Knife

You were what made us cry
in the light to start with
we could see you were there
and we saw what you were
we were hiding from you
and would have been happy
to go on with the dream
that you could not find us
cold flame sight without eyes
line where both shores the seen
and the unseen come down
into nothing to pass
between to separate
to open to divide
what had been once from what
once it had been to tell
apart bringing always
the touch of the present
though the dread of you flares
up far ahead of you
and the memory of
you lingers and goes on
burning ahead of you
we plead with you who have
no ears for us we beg
in private and in vain
do not see us at all
ever we are not here
or if you see us do
not touch us wherever you
were going to touch us
or if you do touch us

divide us from something
it would be good to lose
and save us for ourselves

To Prose

Whatever you may say
whatever you pretend
you do not begin or end
when the stories do
the ones that you repeat
later starting again
or when the days that you tell
all those that never
themselves said a word
have long been utterly still
and yet you were there
when they were
you were heard
commenting in the unmetered
service of understanding
your description
remains current for some time
after the face has gone
even if not written down
but you are different
from what you recount
and although we know
only scattered fragments of you
glimpses of birds in bushes
gestures in car windows
of which we forget
at once almost everything
you define us
we are the ones who need you
we can no longer tell
whether we believe
anything without you

or whether we can hear
all that you are not
O web of answer
sea of forgetting is it true
that you remember

To Duty

Oh dear

where do you keep yourself
whose least footstep wakens
all those sentences
that begin *I thought*

what makes you so sure
as you lay claim
to the cloudless sky of morning

assuming the grammar of the hours
and whatever they
are supposed to be saying
even if we try
to imagine what life
would be like without you

you who do not
seem to listen
you who insist
without a sound
you who know better

even better you say
than nature herself

you who tell us
over and over
who we are

To Billy's Car

You were not going anywhere
any more

with your nose to the wall
and your cracked tires
but it seems you went just the same
and nobody noticed

by then we ourselves had gone
from the smell of your mildewed velvets
and the mica hue of the world
through your windows after supper
and the touch of your numb controls

by then the model airplanes
I suppose were no longer turning
on their strings under the ceiling
of the silent room kept
the way Billy's dead brother had left it
and his grandmother had stopped
baking cakes and crying
at all the dying
she kept mumbling over

and by that time no doubt
the girl we talked about
with whom we were both in love
who went to a different school
so that we never saw her
except in the choir on Sunday
had married somebody else
with a lot of money

looking through your old windshield
that had been there all winter
we could see the grass
that was growing on the wall that year
as we went on talking
into the spring evening

To the Present Visitors

Now we come to the famous classroom
where every year a fortunate few
in the days of their youth study
autumn forgetting the numbers beforehand
as they have been doing since the words
were all in Latin no cameras
allowed in here notice the slight breeze
from the windows here among the trees
and the fragrance at the end of spring
notice the leaves outside the window frames
the new grass in the light of morning
notice the charts of colors on the walls
set in order and the moons in the calendars
the constellations the dark dials
the portraits of flowers still as the tables
here they study what is too far away
ever to grasp and too near to recognize
notice the leaves changing as we watch
then it will be summer and these studies
will be over and then it will be autumn
and most of them will be forgotten
notice the bell in place outside the door
and the dog lying near the foot of the stairs
waiting for a time that she remembers

To the Present Tense

By the time you are
by the time you come to be
by the time you read this
by the time you are written
by the time you forget
by the time you are water through fingers
by the time you are taken for granted
by the time it hurts
by the time it goes on hurting
by the time there are no words for you
by the time you remember
but without the names
by the time you are in the papers
and on the telephone
passing unnoticed there too

who is it
to whom you come
before whose very eyes
you are disappearing
without making yourself known

To the Air

Just when I needed you
there you were
I cannot say
how long you had been
present all at once
color of the day
as it comes to be seen
color of before
face of forgetting
color of heaven
out of sight within
myself leaving me
all the time only
to return without
question never
could I live without you
never have you
belonged to me
never do I want
you not to be with me
you who have been
the breath of everyone
and of each word spoken
without needing to know
the meaning of any of them
or who was speaking
when you are the wind
where do you start from
when you are still
where do you go
you who became
all the names I have known

and the lives in which
they came and went
invisible friend
go on telling me
again again

To Muku Dreaming

There in that place
where you are running
are you alone now

you who always know
who is there

there in the place your feet
are touching
are you far from home
you who always know where you are
sleeping and waking

there in the place
where you can see
I see nothing at all
though this day is still here
in which I see you asleep

there where you can hear
I hear nothing
not that the sky is silent

how far do you know
our way
the first time

there when you see
us walking

you who have known all along
that we were there
you see that we

do not have to get anywhere

To the Dust of the Road

And in the morning you are up again
with the way leading through you for a while
longer if the wind is motionless when
the cars reach where the asphalt ends a mile
or so below the main road and the wave
you rise into is different every time
and you are one with it until you have
made your way up to the top of your climb
and brightened in that moment of that day
and then you turn as when you rose before
in fire or wind from the ends of the earth
to pause here and you seem to drift away
on into nothing to lie down once more
until another breath brings you to birth

To That Stretch of Canal

Spring is here dearie I seen a robin up
the canal this morning froze to death
CANAL NEIGHBOR

By now the towpath leads on without you
who were the only reason it was there
in the days that went on barges when you
were young and they vanished on the long sky where
you carried them and when I first saw you
nothing was left of them except that sky
in your later life when I would know you
on summer evenings watching swallows fly
low to your surface and when ice held you
all winter though you were slipping away
even then and what now remains of you
but this long dry grave a shallow valley
and shreds of marsh in the last tracks of you
with things still waving that were thrown away

To the Blue Stork

How strange to have flown so far
beyond seasons and continents
through all those generations
and the stories about you
not one of them ever true
since there was no one who knew you
or the blue you remembered

to find yourself with one eye
looking out at a city
from a picture of you standing
on the side of a black truck
with the other eye invisible
keeping watch on the darkness

and over you those letters
pretending to be yours
nothing to do with you
saying *Blue Coal* although
it was the night's own color
and only its flame was blue
other letters under you

called you *The Smokeless Fuel*
one more story about you
then in quotes as though you
had said it *You Scratch My Back
I'll Scratch Yours* but I knew
that never came from you

O smokeless hue it was you
alone I believed and not
anything said about you

it was your eye that I watched
as it watched the shining day
turning to sky it was you
who could see it was burning

To the Sound of the Gate

Hinge squeak and the small groan
of the spring turning in sleep
both wakened by the cluck
of the latch tongue
and the gate opening

long after the gate is gone
and the fence down
all the square pickets each one
and the shadows in between
painted green over brown
through the summer afternoon

vanished in midair
at Fourth Street by the corner
and inside the gate
that is not there
the flight of steps to the front door
gone and the door they climbed to
and the garden etched on its window
sealed up and shingled over

only the sound of you opening
is still there

To the Stone Paddock by the Far Barn

There where you
had been set down as deep
as a large room into the ridge
like a squared step
rimmed on the low sides
with remnants of walls
lined up on the ledge
high above the river
in another time
and with age the veteran faces
of limestone had lichened
and weathered in their places

I came upon you
many lives further on
when the hands that had heaved
the stones onto each other
and the feet that had stepped
over the sills
set in your west and north walls
the heads that had turned there
and the syllables they had raised
into their weather
had been forgotten
and wars had passed
into clouds on the far ridges
and no one had come back
and brambles had buried you

I was a child when I found you
it seems to me now
in ignorance I came

to the summer blackberries
ripening before me
that were hiding beneath them
your breathless phrase
of a lost language
and as I let
the late daylight in
I was held where I stood
and started to listen

days seasons and years
I have sat in the shade
of your south wall
while the light rolled
over the valley
quince petals still float
across the spring morning there
and the weasel ripples
along the ivy
on your east wall
and in the woods beyond it
birds sing in the hawthorns
in the oaks and bird cherries
autumn brings the scent
of earth and black currants
and the quick bark of the fox
frost creaks in your winter grass

I have imagined staying
there while the walls fell
around me
cradled in the sound of you

To a Few Cherries

Peter and I are up where the branches
sink and swing out underfoot as though they
were not anchored and with the lightest breeze
the limb one hand is holding pulls away
like someone being called but we go on
reaching higher into the leaves where they
shimmer against the light toward a dark one
set among them for the sweetest they say
are those highest up and now the season
is over the last are the best and we
are eating more as we climb drunk on you
laughing but old Delsol warns us from down
below *Don't trust that tree* until we leave you
untasted for all the rest of the story

To My Mother

This very evening I reach
the age you were when you died
I look through the decades
down past the layers of cloud
you had been watching the dark
autumn sky over the garden
and had told me months before
with a grace note of surprise
that you were an old woman
and you laughed at the sound of it
all my life you had told me
that dying did not frighten you
yours was the voice that told me
that I was not afraid
you stood up to go in
knowing it would rain that night

you had seen death many times
before I ever knew you
I am watching the rain now
fall on another garden
I hear your words in my head
it was the winter solstice
before I was thirty
that I was the age you had been
on the day I was born
to slip between numbers
through the measureless days

To My Grandfathers

You who never laid eyes on each other
only one of whom I met only once
and he was the one whose wife could never
forgive him neither would most of their sons
and daughters for the red list of his sins
mainly drink and slipping off downriver
to leave them and live to be a nuisance
out in a shed that time I was brought over
to meet him before they took him away
and you who died when my mother was four
with your fond hopes your wing collar and your
Bessie there was nothing you had to say
to each other to form an influence
soundless as that of planets in their distance

To My Aunt Margie

How could we tell what neither of us knew
that summer morning long ago when I
was a child dressed and combed for meeting you
whose name had floated like part of the sky
over me since before I heard it my
mother's one revered older cousin who
never had married but taught school and by
that time had retired to the hotel you
had for your palace snowcapped majesty
before the fall you came to stay with us
and we took walks in the cemetery
with our dog and when you died you left me
all you had and it bought me the old house
that claimed me on first sight as it still does

To My Father's Houses

Each of you must have looked like hope to him
once at least however long it lasted
he who claimed he saw hope in every grim
eyeless gray farmhouse uninhabited
on a back road and hope surely was needed
every time they were shown into the bare
resonant rooms of the manse provided
by his next church and looked around to where
their lives would wake and they would never own
where they woke and he managed to buy you
never to live in though he thought he might
and projected you onto his days one
by one in the borrowed house they came to
for the last years until the sheet went white

To My Brother

Our mother wrote to you
before you were born
a note you might open
at some later date
in case she should not
be there to tell you
what was in her mind
about wanting you
when she had not seen you

that was before
my time and it
never turned out like that
you never saw the letter
and she never saw you
who were perfect they said
and dead within minutes
that far ahead
of me and always
looking the other way
and I would be the one
to open the letter
after she was gone

and you had answered it
without a word
before I was there
to find out about you
unseen elder
you perfect one
firstborn

To Micky

Since you have come now
to remember nothing
tell me at any rate
what you have forgotten
however it may have gone
for you are the only one
left who still had
all of it in your head
whatever it all
may have amounted to
and you looked after it
there I suppose the way
you took care of everything
and of everybody in turn
without a word about it
for you seemed to be able
to lay hands on anything
I happened to ask you about
when I had the sense to ask
Harry building dance platforms
along the river some time
back before Admiral Dewey
and what drove your sister
during another war
to jump from the Ford City bridge
and Dutch withered in age
with crayons melted in her hair
from sleeping against the steam pipe
the year the boiler froze
was that all it came down to
those bits you found for me
I may as well ask you
only you would know

To Doris

If I had seen this silk
when it mattered to you
in the way that the long
parade of that nature

caught your eye and held you
coaxing you to covet
one after the other
for years those flowers of

no season which enticed
you to imagine their
still petals that recur
in these profuse patterns

of finished artifice
as a veil hovering
about some figure of
yourself suggesting you

behind flowers of silk
on a black ground I would
have found these peonies
of a distant time these

colors motionless on
black less clear than they are
now that you are not here
who wanted to wear them

To the Old

By now you could almost
be anyone and by now
it seems that is who you are

when did it happen
when did it
come to pass
unperceived in spite
of the warnings of a lifetime

surely it was not so
that summer day arched
above the shallow
stream over your shadow
to see the transparent fish
flash beneath your face
they are still flying there
silent in the same sky
where no one else sees them

surely it was not so
when first your fingers
listened under clothing
to the skin calling to you
over the hills
as you still hear it
far away only you

where now
are the questions
that you alone can answer
are they old enough yet

to know who you are
have they heard that you
are still here
do they have the words
would they recognize you

you who could almost be no one

To the Dog Stars

But there is only one of you
they say as though they knew
and it may even be true
one moment at a time
along the journey of light
yet they keep finding you
farther and farther shining
from before they believed you
or ever could have seen you
burning before and after
anything they could have known
each one the only direction
and they have no names for you

although we cannot see through
the transparent days
we go on following you
out of the flash of childhood
out of the blaze of youth
out of the lights we knew
we have been following you

after father and mother
and all the faces we came to
and the eyes that we saw through
our breath the beat of our blood
the soles of our feet our hair
go on following you

To the Tray Dancers

None of the words drifting
across the upturned faces
down in the packed street
was meant for your ears
all the way up there
too high to believe
on that June morning
in the strange city
the year I was nine
all the words were saying hush
whatever they were saying
as we stood watching you
up on the roof of the hotel
that seemed even taller
than it looked in the post cards
could you be real at all
so high and small and far
from who we thought we were
you seemed to move more slowly
than we did down here
you in the shining gown
you in the black suit and top hat
raising your hands once
then turning to the ladder
that rose from behind you
and spidering all the way
up the high pole to the round
tea tray there on top
while a drum rolled until
first one then both of you
stood on the tray up there
in the clouds and daylight

and you raised your hands again
then the music began
and you started to dance
revolving together
turning around and
around on the tray
arms out over air
heads thrown back as you whirled
and where were we all that time
what were we standing on
with our terrors spinning
on top of the pole
while the music went on
and when it stopped
we knew we were falling
until we saw you climb down
toward the lives waiting
at the foot of the air
where a whisper began
that it was all an act
to sell some brand of shoes
but you bowed and were gone
and left us as we had been

To the Mistakes

You are the ones who
were not recognized
in time although you
may have been waiting
in full sight in broad
day from the first step
that set out toward you
and although you may
have been prophesied
hung round with warnings
had your big pictures
in all the papers
yet in the flesh you
did not look like that
each of you in turn
seemed like no one else
you are the ones
who are really my own
never will leave me
forever after
or ever belong
to anyone else
you are the ones I
must have needed
the ones who led me
in spite of all
that was said about you
you placed my footsteps
on the only way

To Luck

In the cards and at the bend in the road
we never saw you
in the womb and in the cross fire
in the numbers
whatever you had your hand in
which was everything
we were told never
to put our faith in you
but to bow to you humbly after all
because in the end there was nothing
else we could do

but we were not to believe in you

and though we might coax you with pebbles
kept warm in the hand
or coins or relics
of vanished animals
observances rituals
none of them binding upon you
who make no promises
we might do such things only
not to neglect you
and risk your disfavor
O you who are never the same
who are secret as the day when it comes
you whom we explain
whenever we can
without understanding

To the Blank Spaces

For longer than by now I can believe
I assumed that you had nothing to do
with one another I thought you had arrived
      whenever that had been

more solitary than single snowflakes
with no acquaintance or understanding
running among you guiding your footsteps
      somewhere ahead of me

in your own time O white lakes on the maps
that I copied and gaps on the paper
for the names that were to appear in them
      sometimes a doorway or

window sometimes an eye sometimes waking
without knowing the place in the whole night
I might have guessed from the order in which
      you turned up before me

and from the way I kept looking at you
as though I recognized something in you
that you were all words out of one language
      tracks of the same creature

To the Morning (1)

Was there once a day when I knew what to ask
looking into the bright hour while it was arrayed before me
were there actual words of the only language
native to that hour and to me that rose unbidden by thought
gone at once taken by the moment as it heard them
while the shadow moved unperceived and the breath
went with its sails and the faces turned and were
there no longer though the love was still talking to them
as it is still talking to them while the rooms fade and dissolve
and the houses turn into seasons and now when so much has
vanished is it possible that in some other time
I knew how to speak of you early light
breeze in the garden toward the end of a year together
in which we wake remembering
or did you come by yourself without anyone knowing your name

To Monday

Once you arrive it is plain
that you do not remember
the last time

you are always
like that
insisting upon
beginning
upon it all beginning
over again
as though nothing had really happened
as though beginning
went on and on
as though it were everything
until it had begun

you never know who you are
the hands of the clock find you
and keep going
without recognition
though what your light
reveals when it rises
wakes from another time
which you appear to have forgotten

travelling all that way
blank and nowhere
before you came to be
with the demands
that you bring with you
from the beginning

each time it is
as though you were the same
or almost
O unrepeatable one
needing nothing yourself
and not waiting

To the Long Table

The sun was touching the wet black shoulders of olives
in a chipped dish descended from another century
on that day I remember more than half my life ago
and you had been covered with a tablecloth of worn damask
for lunch out on the balcony overhanging the stream
with the grapes still small among the vine leaves above us
and near the olives a pitcher of thin black acrid wine
from the cellar just below and an omelette on a cracked white platter
a wheel of bread goat cheeses salad I forget what else
the ducks were asleep down on the far side of the green pond
Jacques came and went babbling fussing making his bad jokes
boasting about old days that nobody else remembered
the lacquered carriages the plumes on the horses and what his mother
had replied to the admiral whose attentions amused her
all the castles they had lost before he had grown up
and when the meal was over he said you too were for sale
he had discovered you in a carpenter's shop
where you had been used as a workbench without regard
for your true worth and the scars on you came from there
your history without words upon which words have gathered

To the Margin

Following the black
footprints the tracks
of words that have passed that way
before me I come
again and again to
your blank shore

not the end yet
but there is nothing more
to be seen there
to be read to be followed
to be understood
and each time I turn
back to go on
in the same way
that I draw the next breath

the wider you are
the emptier and the more
innocent of any
signal the more
precious the text
feels to me as I make
my way through it reminding
myself listening
for any sound from you

To the Middle

O you who pass like a day and never
a soul that sees you guesses who you are
as you go until the rest is over
if someone happens to look back that far
how could you have been known when once you came
unannounced and transparent as the air
at different times for each one yet the same
each one must think as you slip by them there
as the moment before and the next one
which makes no sign that you have come and gone
you upon whom all time and battles turn
so it appears that you are here always
a stillness in the passage of the days
around which the ages of heaven burn

To the Next Time

Knowing as I do
that you will not be there
whenever it may be
that I imagine you
I go on even so
day after day as though
I might believe in you

with your unseen stars again
back at home in the places
they had moved away from
already by the time
I could remember them
and my age what it was
whenever it may have been
that I looked forward from
to you as though that time
when it was there were less
believable less true
and less present than you

so that even if you
occurred and were the same
you could not help but be
different in your way
while any temporary
moment I live through
may still seem to be
a passing sketch of you
as you were meant to be
this time this time

To the Light of September

When you are already here
you appear to be only
a name that tells of you
whether you are present or not

and for now it seems as though
you are still summer
still the high familiar
endless summer
yet with a glint
of bronze in the chill mornings
and the late yellow petals
of the mullein fluttering
on the stalks that lean
over their broken
shadows across the cracked ground

but they all know
that you have come
the seed heads of the sage
the whispering birds
with nowhere to hide you
to keep you for later

you
who fly with them

you who are neither
before nor after
you who arrive

with blue plums
that have fallen through the night

perfect in the dew

September 10, 2001

To the Words

When it happens you are not there

O you beyond numbers
beyond recollection
passed on from breath to breath
given again
from day to day from age
to age
charged with knowledge
knowing nothing

indifferent elders
indispensable and sleepless

keepers of our names
before ever we came
to be called by them

you that were
formed to begin with
you that were cried out
you that were spoken
to begin with
to say what could not be said

ancient precious
and helpless ones

say it

September 17, 2001

To the Grass of Autumn

You could never believe
it would come to this
one still morning
when before you noticed
the birds already
were all but gone

even though year upon year
the rehearsal of it
must have surprised
your speechless parents
and unknown antecedents
long ago gathered to dust
and though even the children
have been taught how to say
the word *withereth*

no you were known to be
cool and countless
the bright vision on all
the green hills
rippling in unmeasured waves
through the days in flower

now you are as the fog
that sifts among you
gray in the chill daybreak
the voles scratch the dry earth
around your roots
hoping to find something
before winter
and when the white air stirs

you whisper to yourselves
without expectation
or the need to know

September 18, 2001

To Ashes

All the green trees bring
their rings to you
the widening
circles of their years to you
late and soon casting
down their crowns into
you at once they are gone
not to appear
as themselves again

O season of your own

from whom now even
the fire has moved on
out of the green voices
and the days of summer
out of the spoken
names and the words between them
the mingled nights the hands
the hope the faces
those circling ages dancing
in flames as we see now
afterward
here before you

O you with no
beginning that we can conceive of
no end that we can foresee
you of whom once we were made
before we knew ourselves

in this season of our own

September 19, 2001

To Zbigniew Herbert's Bicycle

Since he never
really possessed you
however he may have longed to
in secret

so that in dreams he knew
each surface and detail of you
gleam of spokes and chrome
smells of grease and rubber
the chain's black knuckles

day by day you
remained out of sight
so that he never had to
lock you up or hide you
because nobody could see you

and though he never
in fact learned how to ride you
keeping his round
toppling weight upright
on the two small toes
of water slipping
out from under

once he was well away
hands on the grips feet off the ground
you could take him
anywhere

at last like the rain
through the rain

invisible as you were

September 21, 2001

To the Coming Winter

Sometime after eleven the fireworks
of the last fête of this autumn begin
popping down in the valley a few sparks
here and there climbing slowly through thin rain
into the darkness until they are gone
above the carnival din and the caught
faces lit by wheeling rides in that one
moment looking up still and shining what
are they celebrating now that the fine
days are finished and the old leaves falling
and fields empty this year when a season
has ended and we stand again watching
those brief flares in the silence of heaven
without knowing what they are signalling

September 23, 2001

To the Smell of Water

But is it really you
behind the pretenses
beyond dust and distances
beneath the salt and the siren
announcements and ancient
impurities and decays
that claim to be you

we have thought we knew you
emerging around us
as we came to the lake
and racing by us
as we listened to the river
and reminding us
from the ends of the streets
and waving across the boardwalk
and along the sand
and hovering above the clear glass

as a child I ran to you
with a pounding heart
and out in the desert
the camel turns to you
and the rain at night
falls through you

yet it is said that none
of the breaths that we
believe to be you
is really your own
for you have none
that is yours alone

and what we take to be
you is only
what is told about you
while you remain
apart from it like our days
our nights our years

To the Beginning of Rain

You never guessed
that anyone was watching

I knew you were on the way
I wondered how long it would be
until you appeared
falling before there was
any knowledge of falling
falling with no way of knowing

without why or where
pure falling
what is it
like

even from here
I can tell for an instant
it is not like anything

the color of air
but not air
nor like air
the color of leaves and their shadows
passing through them as though
they were not there
color of the sight of an eye
moving across the eye but
not remembering it

color of light at this moment
but not light
color of going

as it goes
color of not knowing
as it went

To a Mosquito

Listen to you
me me me
nothing but *me*
even without a voice
and rash though it may be

to sing out anyway
here I am this is me
out for your blood

do you mean to tell me
we are some kind of kin
blood relatives
your many offspring
something to me
by blood presumably
but with the gift of flight

on wings as fine
as light glinting across water
and with the deaths they carry

you need not tell me
that you are here
because of me
you follow me everywhere
by my breath you find me
by the life of my body
you hunger to be close to me
whatever I am doing

though we do not take
each other personally
you recognize me
I make the world right for you
it is as though you
believe I owe you something

To Glass

Which of you was first
you or the days

at pretending not
to be visible
to be there but not visible

by fire out of sand

which of you first
started to look
like the other

and to look like
the air
and the hour
and the colored light
that you allow us
to see through you
to recognize the day
turning out of reach

while you appear to be
stillness itself
no one at all
holding in place

the promise
of the known world
on the other side

which the birds fly into
the last time

To Purity

I have heard so much about you

if you claim to be you
I will know it is not true

if you say nothing I will listen
as I do
with my own
old mixed feelings
of hope and reservation

hearing through them
whatever might be you

the way I see
the white light from
the beginning
through the colors of the garden
through a face an eye

To Salt

Taste of taste

you that know without saying

you that also began somewhere in the light
as a dust
in the light
long before anything could have tasted you
before anything could have recognized you
traveller through the dark through the earth through the sea
finding your way in time into sweat and blood
and into tears that we know as our own
or another's

O great silent teacher whose scripture we fulfill
you that made us able to taste you

you lead us to the light and to the darkness
you teach us the coming and going of each other
you wake us with joy and pain and terror
one at a time or all together
as long as we recognize you

as long as we know
the touch of you on our lips

To the Lightning

Now I can believe
that you never left

that always you
were there outside time
thinking in the dark
a moment of the world
waking it
to its only instant
changing it
even before it knew

ancestor

whom your children
have never remembered
not one of them
and whose illumination
they could not hope to survive

beginning

around us all that time
unchanged as we travelled
from whom our eyes are descended
and the things we say

whenever we see you
there is a question
we do not dare to remember

and you disappear
before there are words for it

is that from you too

To the Escape of Light

How late
was it
could you tell

by the time
rhyme came
to occur as though
it might be your shadow
in flight
your echo

O you
who began far
beyond what you
knew

all at once
out of the utter
darkness that no one
could be said to know

showing
yourself where
you would go
as you
appeared there

for the only time
how long can you
go on guiding
yourself through

darkness into
darkness as though
you knew

To a Leaf Falling in Winter

At sundown when a day's words
have gathered at the feet of the trees
lining up in silence
to enter the long corridors
of the roots into which they
pass one by one thinking
that they remember the place
as they feel themselves climbing
away from their only sound
while they are being forgotten
by their bright circumstances
they rise through all of the rings
listening again
afterward as they
listened once and they come
to where the leaves used to live
during their lives but have gone now
and they too take the next step
beyond the reach of meaning

To the Fire

How long I have been
looking into you
staring through you into
the other side
there is no way of telling

it appears to have continued
from an age of its own
this scrutiny of the bright
veil rising and the lit
corridors of the embers
in which I see the days

beyond touch beyond reach
beyond all understanding
beyond their faces
beneath your dangerous wings
you at whose touch
everything changes
you who never change

there in you one at a time
are days unknown
turning the corners
and the unseen past
the unrecognized present
familiar but already
beyond identity

expressions without selves
appearing finally within you
of whom the light is made

To Smoke

Even now when we
can no longer remember
how much of the scent
of the world we gave up
life after life in the hope
of being able to hold
something in our hands

we recognize you at once
every time without fail
day or night wherever
you may be coming from
across the hill or
under the door
and we imagine you
even when you are not there
we can never be sure
you reach all the way to us
out of somewhere we have forgotten
we wake into dreams of you
as the bees do
hoping it is not true

the world is burning
you have always been warning
us too late and only
as you were leaving
ghost of what we have known
something reminds us of you
in the fragrance of morning
in the opening flowers
in a breath at the moment
when it seems to be ours

To Forgetting

Queen of the night
whose reign began
before
always before
mother of how
the story goes
song older than singing

you sweep up my footsteps
how did I find my way here
now there is no way back
you blow my words away
without my hearing you

you erase the faces
even of the living
you travel backward
wherever you are going
taking the days with you
all of them
even the ones I imagined
were safe forever

sovereign of terrible freedom
O you without feature
and without end
whose face I never see
or never remember
how can I love you

except when you appear
for a moment wearing

the veils and the long train
of memory

disguised as memory
the queen of the day

To the Wires Overhead

This is the year
when the swallows did not come back

you have not noticed

now all spring
the evening messages
are no longer passing through
the feet of swallows
lined up in a row
holding you
under the high
strung sparks of their voices

with the notes of that
music changing
as once more they would go
sailing out and once more
singly or in pairs or
several together
across the long light they would
skim low over the gardens
and down the steep pastures
and over the river
and would come back to their places
to go on telling
what was there while it was there

you do not hear
what is missing

To a Tortoiseshell Lyre

Do you know how beautiful you are
did you ever know such a thing

O hollow cradle of light
large as an empty embrace
shape of old waves
and of supplication and offering
fashioned out of all
the ambers of memory

here at the center
at the deepest part
where your heart has been
the notes were plucked
once according to
a time of music
to accompany the singing
that someone claimed
would be here forever

here your heart began
as an echo
in answer to the sea
here once you heard
how the light came through it

To the Gods

When did you stop
telling us what we could believe

when did you take that one step
only one
above
all that

as once you stepped
out of each of the stories
about you one after the other
and out of whatever
we imagined we knew
of you

who were the light
to begin with
and all of the darkness
at the same time
and the voice in them
calling crying
and the enormous answer
neither coming nor going
but too fast to hear

you let us believe
the names for you
whenever we heard them
you let us believe the stories
how death came to be
how the light happened

how the beginning began
you let us believe
all that

then you let us believe
that we had invented you
and that we no longer
believed in you
and that you were only stories
that we did not believe

you with no
moment for beginning
no place to end
one step above
all that

listen to us
wait
believe in us

To the Veil

Small mist
suddenly on the windshield
reflection of an unseen field
of lavender in the air
not flowering there

patch of translucent
uncolored twilight
after the day of color

dazzling shadow
how
have I come to know you

as when a forgotten
dream returns
to stand in the daylight

neither appearing nor
disappearing
in front of the day
like the day itself

constantly unforeseen
and yet recognized
as though it had long been known

To the Way Back

If you can be said
to remember

and by that I mean
if you
can be said to remember

anything

if you
can be
said to be
anything

remember how
you came to be
how you came
to pass

remember who it was
in whose feet
you took the first steps

that was me
not watching
to see whether
you were there

not waiting for you
don't forget
the way back my
mother said

not forgetting you
forgetting you
in the dark of the shoes
in the sounds of the stairs
in the opening door

now that you
have not been there
for so long
do you remember
where you were
before I turned
to look for you

To the Thief at the Airport

Disciple of not knowing
your face keeps reappearing
out of its shady morning
among the cars and saying
that used phrase about looking
for where you were not going

thin smoke for your vanishing

in the moment revealing
suddenly what was missing
the clasped tender of being
someone all the cards telling
the dates and places giving
numbers pictures everything

without even mentioning

those worn familiars each thing
beyond price and worth nothing
from their new absence mocking
any thought of replacing
by then they had no meaning
wherever you were hiding

where your prayers had been leading

to that moment not knowing
what it was you were holding
under your sweater breathing
to the night of not knowing
to contain you like nothing
so you could go on living

To the Afterlife

The way we talk

before those who we tell ourselves
do not hear us

is that really the way
we talk the rest of the time
how can we ever be sure of it
once we start listening
to ourselves as we do
when we talk in front of you

and when are you not there

how old you must be
who do not sleep
and never meet our eyes
though you are never out of them
you who were not born

if you do not hear us
we can ask anything of you

listen

now in the still night
the sound of breathing
remember it
whether you hear it or not

To Finding Again

Everything else must have changed
must be different
by the time you appear
more than ever the same

taking me by surprise
in my difference
my age
long after I had come
to the end
of believing in you
to the end of hope

which was not even
the first of the changes

when I imagined
that I was forgetting you
you did not even need memory
to remain there
letting the years vanish
the miles depart

nothing surprising in that

even longing
does not need memory
to know what to reach for

and nothing surprises you
who were always there
wherever it was

beyond belief

To the Surgeon Kevin Lin

Besides these words that are made of
breath and memory with features
of both and are only mine as
   I address them to you

what do I owe to that steady
fire I watched burning behind your
glasses through the dire spelling-out
   when we met that first day

and to the passion of the boy
from Taiwan and the sharp knowledge
it burned a way to until it
   stood before the open

red cavern and between pulses
was sure how to do what came next
had it not been for that would I
   have been here this morning

at home after a night's rain as
the first sunlight touches the drops
at the tips of the leaves I owe
   you the sight of morning

To Days of Winter

Not enough has been said
ever in your praise
hushed mornings
before the year turns new
and for a while afterward
passing behind the sounds

Oh light worn thin
until the eye can
almost see through you
still words continuing
to bloom out of yourselves
in the way of the older stars
your ancestors

season from before knowledge
reappearing
days when the sun is loved most

To a Friend Turning Fifty

Peter we talk as though
we knew what the years were
that seem to slip from us
                    even before

they arrive where have they
gone where were they heading
from the beginning where
                    did they start from

before there were numbers
in the hollow with no
circumference that we
                    still feel turning

and keep counting the turns
inventing numerals
to call them by but they
                    leave us the names

which are nothing to them
and what they bring us for
a present is without
                    name or number

unseizable as this
daylight in which the life
you have come to appears
                    to you all at

once congratulations
let the day welcome you
as its guest the way you
            welcome your friends

To Being Late

Again again you are
the right time after all

not according to
however we planned it

unforeseen and yet
only too well known
mislaid horizon
where we come to ourselves
as though we had been expected

you are where it appears now
and will stay from now on
in its own good time
it was you we came to
in the first place
hearing voices around us
before we knew what they said

but you always surprise us
it is you that we
hurry to
while you go on waiting
to the end of space

and when we get to you
we stop and listen
trying to hear whether
you are still there

To the Morning (2)

It does not matter to you
what I fail to understand
as the light enters the sky

you arrive for the first time
knowing everything at once
and offer the beginning
again whether anyone
can see what it is or not
while it is here before us

as though it had always been
here as it is with nothing
forgotten even while you

are turning away again

To the Moss

How you came to know all that you are sure of
how you discovered the darkness of green
uncurling into the daylight out of
its origins unsounded as your own
how you learned to fashion shapes of water
into softness itself that stayed in place
and kept some secret of caves wherever
you were but with such welcome seemed to rise
that in time you became as some believe
a model for the cheek and then the breast
the wren felt she knew most of that before
there were breasts or cheeks and she made out of
living bits of you the globe of her nest
as though that was what you had grown there for

To an Old Acacia

Into the morning fine white rain
keeps drifting along the valley
taking it away already
though it is still spring
with the brief blue flights flashing
to the nest above the kitchen window

and you appear to me again
where you have not stood for so long
wherever we may have been

I see it is evening where you are
though you seem as near
as a figure in the room
all day you have held
a single note of darkness
one rough hollow column
the sound of a breath

neither knowing nor not knowing
through the glare of high summer
and the incandescent cicadas

is the note I remember now
the one that I heard
in those days
when your gnarled branches might still
hold out white flowers
over the dead limbs

when it is night
do you still echo the owl

To the Story

Even now I suppose you are hiding
in the daylight the way you always do
        granting only

the most cursory kind of attention
or none at all like a self off in some
        other country

other time other life as though you knew
better than the moment while the moment
        is quietly

there unproclaimed with its occasions its
events signalling from their distances
        you fail to see

as it passes before you what you will
never manage to remember later
        the missing key

to the present and its unrepeated
life and so you will have to make it up
        as plausibly

as you can out of odds and ends of what
someone wrote down or you may remember
        if memory

serves you or you will conjure from those same
elements and selves summoned out of some
        other country

other time other life some other tale
that never happened to be the truth of
                what could not be

told as it lived and breathed and eluded
our attention as though in itself it
                had no story

To a Dormouse

You never knew how you came by your names
in any language because none was yours
Muscardinus avellanarius
         whom your mother

did not call that nor refer to you as
one of the *Gliridae* it was somewhere
in the north that the word for you first told
         only of your

fondness for sleeping through the world's winter
how did they learn that did anyone come
upon you once before you woke and want
         to remember

something of that time glimpsed from far away
it happens to us too words that pretend
to represent us may at this moment
         be making their

transits from one stranger to another
as though they were uttered during our sleep
and did Buffon himself ever meet you
         who said you were

smaller than squirrels but fatter and not
to be tamed as squirrels might be but with
your teeth would defend yourself to the last
         and he never

said anything of your color like that
of a fawn in the shade nor of your tail
the grace in it the small tuft at the end
            nothing of your

elegant mask nor of the curious
quiet of your eyes their steady lights
awake in their distances over us as
            they would appear

above the curtain rod in the evening
and watch us through dinner and then vanish
but this time when I find you it seems that
            you stayed on there

looking down into the room all winter
empty table plates put away no one
there and you fell asleep into the sleep
            of the future

To the Parting Year

So you are leaving everything
the way it is
taking only your day with you

already you are out of reach
you do not know us or hear us
you scarcely remember us
already we cannot imagine
where you are

what we remember of love is starlight

To the New Year

With what stillness at last
you appear in the valley
your first sunlight reaching down
to touch the tips of a few
high leaves that do not stir
as though they had not noticed
and did not know you at all
then the voice of a dove calls
from far away in itself
to the hush of the morning

so this is the sound of you
here and now whether or not
anyone hears it this is
where we have come with our age
our knowledge such as it is
and our hopes such as they are
invisible before us
untouched and still possible

To the Unfinished

Clear eminence without whom I would be
nothing O great provision never seen
barely acknowledged even wished away
        without thinking

you in whose immeasurable presence
the darkness itself comes to be itself
and light recalls its colors and each sound
        comes echoing

your undertone I have forgotten when
I first woke into knowing you were there
before words ever reached me but that time
        under your wing

is still with me you have carried it all
the way along with faces that surface
appearing almost as they were before
        and with the spring

that returns through its leaves never the same
you have brought me once more to the old house
after all these years of remembering
        without knowing

it was you who kept opening the way
offering me what I had to choose it is
you who come bringing me the only day
        in the morning

To Paula

We keep asking where they have gone
those years we remember and we
reach for them like hands in the night
knowing they must be as close as
that those twenty years that were
just here we did not set them down
no not that first night talking at
Il Monello what did we say
and then the joy of that summer
that became the joy of the years
after it yes that is where they
are they turned into each other
love and all and have turned into
us now the way a journey turns
into the traveller even
as its sequence is forgotten
they turned into this later joy
one day on another island
near the end of another year
wondering what became of them

To Myself

Even when I forget you
I go on looking for you
I believe I would know you
I keep remembering you
sometimes long ago but then
other times I am sure you
were here a moment before
and the air is still alive
around where you were and I
think then I can recognize
you who are always the same
who pretend to be time but
you are not time and who speak
in the words but you are not
what they say you who are not
lost when I do not find you

To the Happy Few

Do you know who you are

O you forever listed
under some other heading
when you are listed at all

you whose addresses
when you have them
are never sold except
for another reason
something else that is
supposed to identify you

who carry no card
stating that you are—
what would it say you were
to someone turning it over
looking perhaps for
a date or for
anything to go by

you with no secret handshake
no proof of membership
no way to prove such a thing
even to yourselves

you without a word
of explanation
and only yourselves
as evidence

To the Book

Go on then
in your own time
this is as far
as I will take you
I am leaving your words with you
as though they had been yours
all the time

of course you are not finished
how can you be finished
when the morning begins again
or the moon rises
even the words are not finished
though they may claim to be

never mind
I will not be
listening when they say
how you should be
different in some way
you will be able to tell them
that the fault was all mine

whoever I was
when I made you up

About the Author

W.S. Merwin was born in New York City in 1927. From 1949 to 1951, he worked as a tutor in France, Majorca, and Portugal; for several years afterward he made the greater part of his living by translating from French, Spanish, Latin, and Portuguese. His many awards include the Pulitzer Prize in Poetry, the Lannan Lifetime Achievement Award, the Tanning Prize for mastery in the art of poetry (now the Wallace Stevens Award), the Bollingen Award, the Ruth Lily Poetry Prize, as well as fellowships from the Rockefeller and the Guggenheim foundations and the National Endowment for the Arts. He is the author of many books of poetry and prose; his most recent volume of poems is *Migration: New & Selected Poems*. For the past thirty years he has lived in Hawaii.

Copper Canyon Press wishes to acknowledge the support of
Lannan Foundation in funding the publication and distribution
of exceptional literary works.

LANNAN LITERARY SELECTIONS 2005

June Jordan, *Directed by Desire*

W.S. Merwin, *Migration*

W.S. Merwin, *Present Company*

Pablo Neruda, *The Separate Rose*

Pablo Neruda, *Still Another Day*

Alberto Ríos, *The Theater of Night*

LANNAN LITERARY SELECTIONS 2000–2004

John Balaban, *Spring Essence:
The Poetry of Hồ Xuân Hương*

Marvin Bell, *Rampant*

Hayden Carruth, *Doctor Jazz*

Cyrus Cassells, *More Than Peace
and Cypresses*

Norman Dubie, *The Mercy Seat:
Collected & New Poems, 1967–2001*

Sascha Feinstein, *Misterioso*

James Galvin, *X: Poems*

Jim Harrison, *The Shape of the Journey:
New and Collected Poems*

Maxine Kumin, *Always Beginning:
Essays on a Life in Poetry*

Ben Lerner, *The Lichtenberg Figures*

Antonio Machado, *Border of a Dream:
Selected Poems,* translated by
Willis Barnstone

W.S. Merwin, *The First Four Books
of Poems*

Cesare Pavese, *Disaffections:
Complete Poems 1930–1950,* translated by
Geoffrey Brock

Antonio Porchia, *Voices,* translated
by W.S. Merwin

Kenneth Rexroth, *The Complete Poems of
Kenneth Rexroth,* edited by Sam Hamill
and Bradford Morrow

Alberto Ríos, *The Smallest Muscle in the
Human Body*

Theodore Roethke, *On Poetry & Craft*

Ann Stanford, *Holding Our Own:
The Selected Poems of Ann Stanford,* edited
by Maxine Scates and David Trinidad

Ruth Stone, *In the Next Galaxy*

Joseph Stroud, *Country of Light*

Rabindranath Tagore, *The Lover of God,*
translated by Tony K. Stewart and
Chase Twichell

*Reversible Monuments: Contemporary
Mexican Poetry,* edited by Mónica de la
Torre and Michael Wiegers

César Vallejo, *The Black Heralds,* translated
by Rebecca Seiferle

Eleanor Rand Wilner, *The Girl with Bees in
Her Hair*

C.D. Wright, *Steal Away:
Selected and New Poems*

For more on the Lannan Literary Selections, visit:

www.coppercanyonpress.org

Copper Canyon Press is grateful to the following individuals and foundations whose extraordinary financial support made publication of this book possible.

Anonymous (5)
David G. Brewster & Mary Kay Sneeringer
Betsey Curran & Jonathan King
Vasiliki Dwyer
Jane W. Ellis & Jack Litewka
The Charles Engelhard Foundation
Kay & Joe Gantt
Mimi Gardner Gates
Stanley & Kip Greenthal
Cynthia Hartwig & Tom Booster
Phyllis Hatfield
George Hitchcock & Marjorie Simon
Steven Holl & Solange Fabiao
Mary Ingraham & Jim Brown
Peter & Johnna Lewis
Sheila & Jim Molnar
Walter Parsons
Cynthia Sears & Frank Buxton
Rick Simonson
Kevin Tighe
Jim & Mary Lou Wickwire
Charles & Barbara Wright

The Chinese character for poetry is made up of two parts: "word" and "temple." It also serves as pressmark for Copper Canyon Press. Founded in 1972, Copper Canyon Press remains dedicated to publishing poetry exclusively, from Nobel laureates to new and emerging authors. The Press thrives with the generous patronage of readers, writers, booksellers, librarians, teachers, students, and funders—everyone who shares the conviction that poetry invigorates the language and sharpens our appreciation of the world.

Major funding has been provided by:

The Paul G. Allen Family Foundation

THE **PAUL G. ALLEN FAMILY** *foundation*

Lannan Foundation

National Endowment for the Arts

Washington State Arts Commission

NATIONAL ENDOWMENT FOR THE ARTS

WASHINGTON STATE ARTS COMMISSION

For information and catalogs:

COPPER CANYON PRESS
Post Office Box 271
Port Townsend, Washington 98368
360-385-4925
www.coppercanyonpress.org